Touched By An
ANGEL

Touched By An Angel

Published by Garborg's, Inc.
P. O. Box 20132, Bloomington, MN 55420

Design by Franke Design Co.

ISBN 1-881830-63-2

What you need to know about the past is that no matter what has happened, it has all worked together to bring you to this very moment. And this is the moment you can choose to make everything new. Right now.

January 1

Sometimes the end is just the beginning, hmmm?

The end is *usually* just the beginning.

December 31

$\mathcal{G}$od is faithful. He will stick with you even when you won't. He will forgive you even when you can't. His mercies are brand new every morning. This morning, He wants to give this day to you, and all the rest of your days, too. All you have to do...is say "yes."

January 2

$\mathcal{G}$od is not the author of confusion.

He likes to write happy endings.

December 30

You don't have to build a building or publish a magazine to make a difference in the world. God can use you right now, where you are, if you will let Him.

January 3

There's gonna be good times.

There's gonna be bad times.

The good Lord can use you all the time.

December 29

*D*on't be afraid. God loves you.

And He has heard your prayer.

January 4

We have been given a marvelous gift. A mystery has occurred in our midst. A holy visitation. We must not greet it with panic and superstition. We must cherish it, and hold it in our hearts until we have learned what God intends for us to do with it.

December 28

Whatever you think you've gotta win, He's already won for you, if you'll just take hold of it. That real prize is God and His love. Set your eyes on that. That's the only thing worth winning.

January 5

Angels do not allow themselves to be the focus of worship. Their purpose is to serve and glorify their Creator.

December 27

$\mathscr{D}$o you know why God put people's faces on the front of their bodies? Faces are in the front so people can see where they're going, not where they've been. We have to go forward, not backward.

January 6

The kingdom of this world is become

The kingdom of our Lord...

And He shall reign forever and ever.

December 26

Faith doesn't get you around trouble,

it gets you through it.

January 7

Hallelujah! For the Lord God Omnipotent reigneth.

December 25

God would never turn His back on you.
Nothing...not death or life or war, not the past, the
present, or the future, no one, no creature on this
earth can ever separate you from God's love.

January 8

And so it was that while they were there the days were accomplished that she should be delivered. She brought forth her first son and wrapped him in swaddling clothes and laid him in a manger, because there was no room for them at the inn.

December 24

There is a difference between what your heart feels and what it knows. Your heart is for holding things: joy, love, pain. But looking to your heart for an answer instead of praying for one can get you into trouble. The answer to prayer comes from God and listening to Him will never trip you up.

January 9

$\mathscr{A}$nd lo, there were in the same country shepherds keeping watch over their flocks by night. And behold, an angel of the Lord stood by them, and the brightness of God showed round about them, and they were greatly afraid, and the angel said unto them. "Fear not, for I bring you good tidings of great joy that shall be unto all people."

December 23

You can't change who you *were*.

But God will help you change who you *are*.

And today, you can start over. Right now.

January 10

Riches cannot always be measured in dollars.

December 22

Has God ever forsaken you? He told you He wouldn't, and He never has. Never. Just because you feel invisible doesn't mean you are.

January 11

$\mathcal{G}$od doesn't give you what you deserve.

He gives you what He wants you to have:

The best of everything, because He loves you.

All you have to do is ask.

December 21

There's a rhythm to life. What we do has eternal consequences, and you've got to have faith that whatever job you're given, it matters.

January 12

You took a gift and let someone ruin it. You sought out fame instead of the needy, you embraced the loud arrogance of pride and became deaf to the tiny voice of a baby in the manger.

December 20

The Almighty God sends angels to this earth,
to bring messages, to comfort, to provide
protection and deliver healing.

January 13

$\mathcal{G}$ive some people a glimpse of heaven and they're off and singing. But some people, you can put heaven right smack in front of 'em, and they still can't see anything to sing about.

December 19

God only knows what's going to happen next."

"Yes...and that's enough."

January 14

*D*o you really think that you have

the power to mess up God's plans?

December 18

$\mathscr{N}$o one really knows you or understands you
completely, except the One who made you.

January 15

When you make mistakes, God will be there
to help you, and forgive you. But you still
must bear the consequences.

December 17

*J*ust keep your heart and your eyes open

and God will show you exactly what to do.

January 16

Some people think they need a lot of things

they don't really need.

December 16

If you can't find the love,

let God love through you.

January 17

You may feel alone, but you're not.

God will not abandon you.

December 15

The trouble with destiny:

You never can dress for it.

January 18

You must never be afraid to ask for what is good and right. You just have to know where to go to ask for it.

December 14

*G*od loves you...because you're you.
You've spent your whole life running and running,
trying to catch up with something that has never
been there for you. And all you've done is go farther
and farther away from the precious love that's
been waiting for you all the time.

January 19

Sometimes you have to stand up and fight for what you believe in. And sometimes it takes even more courage to stay put. To hold your ground and refuse to be bullied.... It doesn't change the bully. But it can change you.

December 13

You've got to decide right now whether the rough times are going to bring you two closer together or pull you apart.

January 20

Hate is like water in a dry river bed.

The longer it runs, the deeper it digs in.

December 12

*P*eople have been painting pictures and writing songs and making movies about heaven ever since they could breathe, but they have never even come close.

January 21

Angels bring messages. They bring comfort.

They can bring protection. They don't heal,

but they can bring healing from God.

December 11

Every little baby is a sign from God

that He hasn't given up on us yet.

January 22

You're not always going to hear the angels. When little children get older, other voices drown the angel voices out. But you should never stop listening for them. Sometimes you'll hear them in the crickets at dusk. Sometimes you'll only hear an angel in the sound of "hello." But never stop listening. And never forget that you did once hear them. And someday, you'll hear them again.

December 10

*W*ho you are is not your name or your family.

Who you are is more essential than that; it comes

from God. And what you make of yourself,

that is what you give back to God.

January 23

Funny thing about a camera.

Captures the moment.

Funny thing about the moment.

There's always a new one.

December 9

Funny, isn't it, how you have to be silent sometimes before you can communicate.

January 24

It's quite a world out there. Disposable careers, disposable wives, disposable faith. But God is not going to let you throw away the gift He's given you.

December 8

Life is a network of invisible threads.

January 25

God would never turn His back on you.

December 7

Dear God, sometimes You arrive with a whisper,

sometimes You fall into our lives. But whatever

You bring to us is beautiful.

January 26

There is love. Share it with everyone

who walks through your door.

December 6

*S*ometimes you need to find the beauty in being alone.

January 27

Everybody's faxing and modeming and onlining and inputting and downloading and overnighting. If you don't like it, change the channel. Press the button. "Escape, Delete." You can send anything to anybody, anywhere in the world in seconds. But it still takes the same time it always took to know a soul, to mend a broken heart...to give birth to a child. Even in a world of change, some things just don't.

December 5

*W*hen you cry, God cries with you.

But He can only wipe your tears if you let Him.

January 28

There's a day that you know changed your life.

And then life gets to be more precious.

December 4

God can always hear you.

January 29

You're having the wrong kind of dreams, man.

You can't waste your time dreaming about the past.

You gotta stick to dreamin' about the future.

December 3

I actually prayed and asked God if just one day

I could do something to make a difference.

Well, you know what they say:

Be careful what you pray for.

January 30

*W*hy would God send an angel to me?...
Just to let you know that there's somebody who's
never going to leave you. That He's going to
love you always. That's His promise.

December 2

You have to have faith that if you've been chosen to do something, God has a very good reason for it.

January 31

This is what you call an unexpected snow. One moment the sky looks clear and the next moment, the sky is falling. And you can run inside and hide, or you can become part of it and let it change you.

December 1

*L*ove doesn't hide. It stays and fights. It goes the

distance. That's why God made love so strong.

So it can carry you...all the way home.

February 1

Sometimes endings are just opportunities.

November 30

It's not something in your genes, like your mother's eyes or your grandmother's nose. No, faith is something you've got to work out for yourself. And it doesn't happen in the good times. Your parents forged their faith, one failure at a time.

February 2

It's a dangerous thing to put people up on a pedestal. Humans have a way of slipping off and landing smack on their faces.

November 29

Shame brings you down.

But true humility will only lift you higher.

February 3

Love, support, and understanding,

that's what families are for.

November 28

The love has always been there for you.

All you needed was the courage

to hold on to it.

February 4

Thank you Lord for this wonderful meal.

And thank you for the hands that prepared it.

And thank you for the hands that share it.

November 27

We can't understand loss.

But we can understand love.

February 5

Thank you, Lord, for this Thanksgiving meal, and thank You for the hands that prepared it. Thank You for all the gifts we take for granted every day, like pumpkins and llamas and stars and snow. Thank You for always remembering the big things, like oxygen and the sun coming up every day, and the little things, like cranberry sauce and fiber optics. Thank you especially for bringing us all here together today.

November 26

God doesn't want to take. He wants to give.

But He can't give you anything 'til

you learn to trust Him.

February 6

Sometimes when the people who love us hurt us,

the only way to find out why is to ask questions.

Maybe you need to look deeper.

November 25

God doesn't expect you to win every time.

He loves you. And you should use that love

to give you the strength to keep going.

February 7

With God, all things are possible.

November 24

There is so much that God wants to show you,

but your fear gets in the way. Give it to Him,

right here, right now.

February 8

There are no tricks to this trade.
Caring and hard work and more caring,
that's what we're here for.

November 23

You can't begin a new life until
you're finished with the old one.

February 9

There are going to be lonely nights ahead,
but when they come I want you to remember that
no matter how lonely you are, you're never alone.

November 22

Evil thrives when good men do nothing.

February 10

You have to be careful what you swear to God,

because He hears you.

November 21

Nothing's more dangerous than loving.
Unless it's not loving. Look, He's not promising
that it's going to be easy, but He says
it's going to be worth it.

February 11

You want a role model? Look a lot higher than some guy who can knock down a three pointer.

Look up. Look all the way up.

November 20

God creates us all in His image.

There are no second-class citizens, no minorities,

no human beings greater or lesser than any other.

We are all the same in His eyes.

February 12

You don't have to be perfect to receive God's love.

November 19

This is the moment of truth. And love is only part
of the truth. And romance...well, romance doesn't
have much to do with either one.

February 13

*A*ngels are messengers of God, not ends in themselves. Angels aren't fairies flapping their wings and granting wishes. God is Someone to reckon with....
Angels don't win. God does. And we do, too.

November 18

Have I told you how much God loves you?

February 14

God doesn't need science to explain Himself.

November 17

It's so easy to go from love to hate.

But from hate back to love,

that's the hard part.

February 15

You never say never in a business like this.

Sometimes the things that you think

will never happen, do.

November 16

Famines, wars, and plagues have wiped out

whole civilizations, but love...love has

never been wiped out.

February 16

There but for the grace of God go I.

November 15

The problem with making heroes out of humans is that when they eventually act like humans, everyone is disappointed.

February 17

Nothing, not death or life or war, not the past,

the present, or the future, no one, no creature on this

earth, can separate you from the love of God.

November 14

*W*herever you go, God is already there.

February 18

God loves you. And He knows the secrets of your heart. But you've let the past come between you and God. Turn the past over to Him. He is strong enough to take it. Give Him your future, too. And He'll make *you* strong enough to face it.

November 13

You don't have to change your life.

Just let God change your heart.

February 19

God loves you. He will not fail you. He wants you

to know that He will walk with you all the way,

but it's up to you to take the first step.

November 12

A perfect little soul doesn't always come

in a perfect little body.

February 20

God wanted your heart to feel, not hide.
He never intended your heart and your mind to
be broken by war. But they were, and you've locked
them away, and now you're afraid if you open the door,
you'll never stop crying. But God made you a
person with tears, too. God loves you.

November 11

Forgiveness won't change the other person.

It will change you.

February 21

The only way to share a friend's pain
is to share their pain.

November 10

$\mathscr{F}$aith is the evidence of things unseen.

February 22

The the thing about the truth is that
it doesn't change and it doesn't go away.

November 9

God never created anything stronger than the power of real love. It lives forever, and you never know where it's coming from next.

February 23

Don't give up now. If God has brought you

this far, He won't leave you. Will you try?

Will you give Him a chance?

November 8

*Sometimes we fear what we can't control,
but God said, "Don't be afraid. I am with you."*

February 24

No matter how hard you try to hide it,

the truth is still the truth.

November 7

*O*nly God has the right to take a life or give one

back. Let Him give yours back to you. Let Him

help you find mercy for those who fail.

February 25

There are rewards out there waiting for you
and bright skies and loving friends and a life so
full you can't even begin to imagine.
Oh, God loves you so much.

November 6

God created you in love. He created your child in love. He will give you the love you need. And then your child will give it back to you, for the rest of your life.

February 26

$\mathscr{N}$ever forget, when you have lost your faith, when God is no longer real to you, go back. Go back to the last place you saw Him. He will be waiting for you there.

November 5

How can you judge something fairly when you don't know what the rules are? You can't play God because you aren't God.

February 27

Good works do not necessarily make a good man.

November 4

What we do in love is never lost.

February 28

God loves you and He knows who you are

no matter what your name is.

November 3

*D*on't worry. It always works out sooner or later.

Cast your cares on God, because He cares for you.

February 29

*W*ith God's help, you can turn judgment into compassion. You can turn hate into forgiveness. And you need to forgive yourself, too.

November 2

*A*ngels don't have any faith at all. Absolutely none.
You see, we don't need it. But you do. That's what
makes you strong. Believing today in the light
that doesn't come until tomorrow.

March 1

$\mathscr{D}$eath.... It's probably the most real thing that
happens on earth. It's awesome and profound, like a
birth. The soul passing from one realm to another.

November 1

When you walk down the road,

heavy burden, heavy load, I will rise and I will walk

with you. When you walk through the night, and you

feel like just giving up the fight, I will comfort you,

and you will rise and I will walk with you.

March 2

*H*ow come you have the power to imagine there are Martians when you don't have the power to imagine there's a God who really exists? A God who loves you. A God who's never forsaken you.

October 31

There's something about the truth.

You never get tired of hearing it.

March 3

Every person must make a choice about
whether to spend their life standing in the darkness
and worrying about all the bad things that might
happen or stepping over into the light and living
their life for the good things.

October 30

Destiny doesn't happen. It arrives.
And when it does, you either batten down
the hatches and wait till it blows over,
or you swing open the gates and
invite it in to supper.

March 4

*A*ngels and proof don't have much in common.

Angels aren't about proof. We're about faith.

Faith is the evidence of things not seen.

October 29

You have the right to be less than perfect.

March 5

You have to do your part. You must tell the truth.

God will take care of you. I promise He will.

October 28

Faith is the most powerful weapon we have.

March 6

Saving lives has its merit, but saving souls

and families and futures, well

there's nothing like it.

October 27

When life keeps you in the dark,

that's when you start looking for stars.

March 7

You've got the most powerful weapon of all.

Love. Stick to it. Evil can't stay around

where there is love.

October 26

Will you wake up and stop just smelling the coffee?

Sooner or later you gotta drink it. It's like life.

You never really know how good it is until you taste it.

March 8

*Marriage is important. Most people
never even know just how important it is.
A happy marriage is a gift from God.*

October 25

Remember, pride goeth before the fall.

March 9

You must be strong now. You must never give up.
And when people make you cry and you're afraid of
the dark, don't forget the light is always there.

October 24

*S*ome of our best living is done

through the people we leave behind.

March 10

*D*id you ever hear the story about the man who was afraid of lions? Well, he was so scared that he ran and he ran and he ran, and he kept looking behind him to see if a lion was catching up to him. And he looked over his shoulder so much he didn't see where he was going. And one day, guess what he ran smack dab into?... A lion.

October 23

In this world, nothing is simple, especially the truth.

People always see to that.

March 11

*Nothing can sneak up on you
when you face it straight on.*

October 22

God gives everyone a purpose.

March 12

Angels, though capable of performing small miracles with the power of God, prefer to rely on truth rather than tricks to make a point.

October 21

There's only one thing in this world that is truly bulletproof. It's faith. The faith you wrap yourself up in every day of your life. Faith that no matter what happens, you won't lose God's love. And all the bullets in the world can't pierce it.

March 13

Grief is a powerful thing. It's a good thing,
a healing thing. It's a way to let go of a lot of pain.
But it's something to go through, not hold on to.

October 20

God loves you. And if God is on

your side, what is there to fear?

Nothing. Now or ever.

March 14

It's hard sometimes. Knowing the what,

but not always knowing the why.

October 19

You'd be surprised Who's around
and Who's listening.

March 15

God's got a plan. It's like the wind; just because you can't see it doesn't mean it's not there.

October 18

God loves you. He loves your family...and all the people whose lives you're about to touch.

March 16

$\mathcal{I}$f you have to lie for something

it will never really be yours.

October 17

God is not taking anything away from you.

The *world* takes things away from us.

God restores them, a thousand times better.

March 17

You can still be somebody. You can.
You can help someone else. It doesn't take
a lifetime. Sometimes it can take just a day.

October 16

$\mathcal{I}$t's time to stop asking "Why me?"

and start asking, "What now?"

March 18

Maybe I came here by mistake, but now

He's given me a new purpose.

October 15

$\mathcal{G}$od is able to heal anything and anyone. He made your body and He can heal your body of any disease. But your body was created to be the temple of something much more precious than physical life. Your body will die someday, somehow. But your spirit, the true you—*that* is where your real life is to be found, and that is what God wants to heal today.

March 19

If you find love, hold onto it, or it'll just slip away.

October 14

*N*othing is impossible, you know.

You can do all things through Him

who gives you strength. Just ask.

March 20

$\mathcal{I}$ didn't think I was lost, but I must have taken a wrong turn somewhere.... You ever wonder how that works? You go right instead of left, you cross the street here instead of there, and then in a second you've changed your life and you don't even know it.

October 13

Most driven people make the mistake of

thinking they're doing the driving.

That's how accidents happen.

March 21

God, sometimes I guess I just take You for granted.
All this work, all the lists, what's it all for without You
right in the middle of it? So, Lord, bless this day.

October 12

God can take the saddest things and turn them into something beautiful.

March 22

You know, it's a funny thing about being afraid.
It has this way of getting in your face so that it's all
that you can see. There's always another choice
out there. But as long as you're afraid,
you'll never be able to see it.

October 11

*B*ad things are always going to happen in life.
People will hurt you. But you can't use that as
an excuse to fail or to hurt someone back.
You'll only hurt yourself.

March 23

Everybody has a hiding place.

October 10

God isn't magic. And neither is the Bible.

Quoting it isn't enough. You've got to live it. From inside.

That's where the changes take place.

March 24

*A*ll your life you've been afraid of life. You'd decide you were too fat or too short or too anything, as long as it could convince you to hide. But God made you and He knew what He was doing.

October 9

*Y*ou exchanged your faith for evidence.
You stopped believing in what you knew, and you

started believing in what you saw. But you see,

faith is the evidence of what you can't see.

March 25

If you truly make a decision
out of nothing but love, it will be a
decision you can live with.

October 8

I've been sent by God to help you through this.

No wings. No halos. Just love. That's what you need.

And that's what God gives.

March 26

The curtain may be coming down on that stage,

but you just remember that with God

you always have an audience.

October 7

Miracles do happen and that's what we're here for.

March 27

My choice of coffee is a good ol' cup of Joe.
Straight ahead. Honest. No camouflage...'cause when
you try to hide what's underneath, you just end
up feeling miserable.

October 6

*D*id you ever point up at the stars and ask

which one God lives on? You're the star.

God lives inside you.

March 28

The most important thing in my life
is not a career. It's you. Who you are,
who you were, who you want to be.

October 5

*S*top listening to fear.

Open up those ears of yours and

listen to the Poet, who is the author

and completer of your faith.

March 29

*D*on't be afraid. God loves you.

So much you can't even imagine it.

October 4

There is a time to live and a time to die.

This is a time to live and love.

March 30

$\mathcal{I}$ don't know where. And I don't know when. The only thing I do know is that the kind of love worth waiting for, you won't have to lie for, or steal, or keep hidden in a box to visit on weekends.

October 3

*A*ngels don't tell you what you should have done.

We're here to tell you that God loves you. And that

He wants you to deal with what you can right now.

Because now is all you can change.

March 31

Nothing can separate you from the love of God.

October 2

$\mathscr{S}$weetheart, we're all on the same team,

trying to win the game together. And don't you

forget who's calling the plays for all of us.

$\mathscr{A}pril\ 1$

None of us knows God's plan. But I do know that when people suffer, God suffers too. And it is in the most difficult of times that people grow the most. If you look to God, He will help you through. And you will discover the strength and courage that He has given you.

October 1

There is no greater love

than to give your life for a friend.

April 2

*Encouragement goes a lot farther
with a person than yelling.*

September 30

You know that God has not left you alone in this.

He does not want you to judge yourself or anyone else.

He wants you to do what you've always done: be His

child and let Him comfort you. Nobody can do

that better than He can right now.

April 3

*T*he miracle is that there isn't more evil

in this world than there is.

September 29

Ask God. He is your helper and He loves you
and He is listening.

April 4

How do people do it? They get up every morning and start all over again. It takes a lot of courage to do that...and they don't even know what angels know.

September 28

Father, forgive me. I forgot my faith in You.

I forgot Your faith in man. I forgot who I am.

April 5

Having seen God and His kingdom, angels already
know what humans must simply have faith in.
It is that quality of faith and the occasional doubts
we must overcome that give humans a strength
that angels can only admire.

September 27

God is not dead. He doesn't die just because you say so. But a part of you dies every time you tell yourself that.

April 6

You may have turned your back on God,

but He's still facing you,

welcoming you.

September 26

Don't worry about what you can't do
or why you can't do it. God can use you.

April 7

God is faithful. He'll forgive you even if you can't.

His mercies are brand new every morning.

And this morning, He wants to forgive you.

All you have to do is say yes.

September 25

God has a plan. And just because you don't
understand it does not mean that
God doesn't understand it.

April 8

*You've got to stop looking at yourself
through your eyes and see yourself
through God's eyes.*

September 24

God loves you and He wants to give you a new name—a name that means victory. True victory, the kind that wins at the game of life.

April 9

*Why is it no one pays attention to the light
until it disappears into the darkness?*

September 23

*The Lord *does* move in mysterious ways.*

April 10

You've always been a child of God, and that should have been enough. But you wanted more. And at what price? What is it going to matter if you gain the whole world and lose your soul?

September 22

The first day one believes can be the most difficult.

And the most beautiful.

April 11

When I get angry, I ask God for patience.

September 21

God has many names, you know. Jehovah, Almighty, Everlasting Father, Alpha and Omega.... But do you know what He calls Himself? "I Am." Ask God who He is and that is what He'll tell you. "I Am." Not "I was," or "I'm going to be." But "I Am." "I Am here for you now because that's where you need me." And if God is here, right here, right now, what is there to fear?

April 12

God has a message for you. He wants you to know that He loves you, that only He can fill that emptiness inside. You just have to open your heart to His truth.

September 20

God can take anything that's broken and make it whole. But you must give Him the pieces, because He's the Creator. And He can take all the pieces and make them fit together.

April 13

God wants you to take your future back while you still have the chance.

September 19

$\mathcal{G}$od loves you, and His love is what
gives you the strength to go on to face
your successes *and* your failures.

April 14

$\mathcal{G}$od doesn't play tricks on people. And He definitely doesn't believe that it's ever too late. You see, with God there is no time. Yesterday, today, and tomorrow all belong to Him, right now. And He's willing to give it all to you, this instant, if you'll accept it.

September 18

*P*eople get very strange when it comes to money.

I'll never understand why they put so

much faith in a piece of paper.

April 15

Don't go questioning what the Lord

has planned for you.

September 17

We feel we have so much to lose in this world. But then you realize if God is there for you, there really isn't that much to lose.

April 16

All the world is not a stage and all the men and women are not merely players. Who you are and what you do matters to God. But how charming you are or how many awards you get is not going to impress the Creator of the Universe. Now you can play all the roles you want, but it doesn't make a lick of difference if you're not playing the one part God wrote for you.

September 16

*H*ate's caused a lot of problems in this world

and it's never solved one yet.

April 17

Frightened people often hide behind anger.

They need understanding.

September 15

*Y*ou ever notice something about humans? You ask them if they could go back and live any day over again, what would they do? It's always to go back and fix something as if they knew precisely the moment when everything went wrong.

April 18

You looked the other way. When people look the other way they can lose a french fry, or they can lose something a lot more precious. Maybe even their soul.

September 14

There are rivers for you to cross, but when
you walk through the waters, God will be with you.
There are mountains for you to climb. But when you
cannot take another step...He will carry you.

April 19

*E*very person on this earth is like a violin. Whatever wood we're made of, whatever unique and distinctive qualities we have, the music is always the purest and the most beautiful when we put ourselves in the hands of the Master.

September 13

When we share our dreams with God, He won't laugh. As a matter of fact, God will take our dreams more seriously than we do, because He knows no compromise. He doesn't deal in pieces of happiness and shadows of dreams. He will ask more of us than we ask of ourselves, but He will return more to us than we could ever hope or imagine ourselves.

April 20

God is not the source of confusion. He is the source and completer of your faith. And that is what you need now. Faith that God knows who you really are. Yes, you are not perfect. No one is perfect. No one. But God's love is perfect. And no one can love us better than He can.

September 12

*P*eople like to think that bad things only happen to faceless strangers in newspapers, until it happens to them. That's why faith must be strong now, *before* we need it.

April 21

Some people think that the word "news" comes from N-E-W-S, North, East, West, and South. It's not true, but it made me think. That's where the news comes from–all the four corners of the world. But where does the truth come from? Some place else entirely.

September 11

God's not a stranger. He's the best friend you've got.

April 22

$\mathcal{I}$f God is willing to forgive you,

who are you not to forgive yourself?

You think you know better than God?

September 10

God can use you right now, where you are,

if you will let Him. You want to know that

you matter. Let Him answer your prayers.

April 23

*Parents and children always see
the past very differently.*

September 9

I just love the way God works.

April 24

No matter what you've done, God loves you.

He wants to take away the hatred you feel for yourself.

He wants to help you set things right.

September 8

Even if you don't believe in God, He believes in you.

April 25

God doesn't care how smart you are.

He cares about what's in your heart.

September 7

You'd be surprised how much baggage people carry around with them. Especially the kind you can't see. Half the time it's filled with the past. And looking inside can be the most important thing a person ever does.

April 26

Why is it that when folks look at an old face

they never see the child inside?

September 6

*W*ho decides what's best? You or God? It's God.

And it's time we asked Him what He wants.

April 27

In Thee, O, Lord, do I take refuge;

let me never be put to shame.

September 5

Every prayer gets answered.

Sometimes the answer is "no."

But sometimes the answer is "not yet."

April 28

God sends angels for many things.

Sometimes to help with life and

sometimes to help with death.

September 4

*S*ecrets are dangerous things.
The closer you hold them, the further away
you push everyone else to keep them safe.

April 29

Let me help you understand something about God.

What's good in the world, God made it. This would

include babies, sunsets, and three-day weekends.

The bad stuff in the world comes from

somebody else entirely.

September 3

In a family, when one person's in trouble,

everyone's in trouble.

April 30

No mistake you may have ever made is bigger

than God's power to fix it.

September 2

If a person walks away from God,

where else is there to go?

May 1

You can't undo anything you've already done, but you can face up to it. You can tell the truth. You can seek forgiveness. And then let God do the rest.

September 1

When we've lost hope, when our hearts
are hard and hopeless, God can soften them and
fill them with hope once again. He is able to do
that. But you have to ask Him to. Right now.
This is your chance to start the miracle.

May 2

There is mercy for you in heaven,

even though it's hard to find on earth.

August 31

If there's anything we should know

it's how delicate life is. How little

things cause big things.

May 3

This is out of my hands now.

But I will be praying for you.

August 30

God loves you.
And He wants to help you

if you'll let Him.

May 4

God loves you and it just breaks

His heart to see you suffer.

You're one of His children.

August 29

*D*ream as big as you can.

But hand those dreams over to God

who really cares about what happens to you.

May 5

You've had setbacks, and you'll have others. It's not important how many times you've fallen. It's how many times you let God pick you up that matters.

August 28

*H*ang in there.

There may be hard times ahead.

But you're gonna get through them,

and He'll be with you all the way.

May 6

There will be another job, but there will never be another family. Someday you're gonna be lying on your deathbed and you aren't gonna be saying, "Gosh, I wish I'd spent more time at the office."

August 27

I have a message for you.

God gave you a job to do. And now God says to you:

"Well done, good and faithful servant."

May 7

We're not here to make it easier.

We're here to make it better.

August 26

$\mathcal{I}$ think the day comes when every daughter

realizes that her mother is more than her mother; she's

another woman with a heart that can be broken too.

May 8

God can't make mistakes or change His mind.

It's not in His nature.

August 25

God has been calling you back.
It was His voice that has always whispered
to you, "Come home. Come home."

May 9

*Y*our son needs to know that you love him, not because he's the best, but because he's your son.

August 24

Every parent makes mistakes. The only one

who hasn't is God. He gave the right child to the right

mother. The best way to thank Him is to honor her.

May 10

I don't know what others will say when they hear the truth, but I know that when you speak it and when you stop hiding and running, your heart and your mind will find peace.

August 23

God turns everything around, all the time,

so something good's got to come out of this....

I just can't tell you when. And remember,

He'll never leave or forsake you.

May 11

When hen two people are on a journey, there will be

miles when they will fall silent, but that doesn't mean

they shouldn't be traveling together.

August 22

$\mathcal{I}$'ve met a lot of men who don't believe in angels,

but I never met a man who didn't *want* to.

May 12

When you stand before God, don't you want
to see the face of a friend instead of a stranger?

August 21

Why is it, if you talk to God, you're praying,

but if God talks to you, you're nuts?

May 13

People are always trying to build a stairway to heaven. Some are like towers, some are only a few steps high. But there's never been one that was high enough to make it all the way to God. That's when a soul has to stand on the top step and call up and say, "Here! Here I am. Please lift me up the rest of the way!" And God hears you. He reaches down and takes you home.

August 20

God has not given you a spirit of fear,
but of power and of love. And He has given
you a sound mind, a good mind.

May 14

Even if every one of your good deeds was a step to heaven, it would never reach high enough.

Only God's mercy can take you there.

August 19

If you commit your heart and your love to someone,
you're afraid that you'll get hurt. Well, you will. Both
of you. You are going to have problems and pain
and anger. You'll also have joy. Great joy.

May 15

God doesn't cause pain. He heals it. He doesn't

hate. He loves. Here's a tip from me to you:

don't blame God for what you don't have.

Thank Him for what you *do* have.

August 18

*S*ometimes things get set in motion that must be

played out. God's timing is not our timing.

May 16

It's dangerous to take pride in the wrong thing.

August 17

We're not here just to save a life.

There are souls involved here.

May 17

God loves all of His creations. And that includes you,

and that includes me. God doesn't leave us when we

mess up. That's when we need Him most, and

He'd never leave us when we need Him.

August 16

*A*ll God asks is that we do our best.

He knows what's in your heart.

May 18

Love may bring people together, but love doesn't always keep them together.

August 15

You don't need proof. You need faith.

May 19

Look, I'll spell it out for you: We mess up sometimes.

You haven't exactly thrown God for a loop, you know.

He can handle it.

August 14

You know, "if" is the saddest word in the history of language. You hold onto that "if" long enough, it can eat a hole right into your heart.

May 20

Hell is separation from God. It's an eternity without light. If you were on your way there, God wasn't sending you. You were sending yourself.

August 13

You fail because you are human,
but God never fails. One way or the other, He
triumphs every time. It's just that humans think
they always have to be there to see it.

May 21

*T*here will be some difficult days,

but your angels are here with you,

and you will not be alone.

August 12

*Sometimes the help we need is
not the help we want.*

May 22

Where is God? He's right here.

Where He's always been!

August 11

Have you ever noticed how even people who don't believe in God find themselves calling out His name in their lowest, loneliest hour? You can't ask for His help unless somewhere, deep down, you truly believe in Him.

May 23

God has a plan. He always does, but sometimes people forget and try to make their own imperfect plans. People can only see a little way down the road. But He can see the whole trip.

August 10

Things happen in God's time, not yours.

May 24

When we ignore the truth, we ignore God,

because God is truth. And what isn't true,

He doesn't want any part of. He can't.

August 9

Nothing meaningful ever really gets forgotten.

It can always be found by those willing to look.

May 25

A coincidence is when God chooses

to remain anonymous.

August 8

The light is always there.

Just ask.

May 26

"Train up a child in the way he should go,

and when he is old he will not depart from it."

God said it and it will happen. Whether

you're there to see it or not.

August 7

The truth may hurt, but it's nothing to fear.

May 27

There's nothing to be afraid of.
On one side, there is life. And on
the other...there is life, too.

August 6

God can do anything. But more importantly,
He always does the right thing. And right now,
He wants to save your life.

May 28

You've been playing hide-and-seek with your life. You cover your eyes thinking no one can see you, that no one will find you. Well, God never lost you.

August 5

Without faith, a man's mind
is nothing but a lonely cell.

May 29

$\mathcal{G}$od said there would be days like this. Days when humans behave so badly to one another that it's all an angel can do to keep loving them. The good news is: that's all you have to do.

August 4

I did something really radical. I prayed.

May 30

Just let yourself be loved.

August 3

No such thing as late.

Destiny picks its own time.

May 31

There are people to cherish and hearts to change.
There is a life to live here. And He will hold your
hand all the way if you will just come into
the light and have faith.

August 2

May the road rise before you...may your swing
be straight...may the ball fly high and far...
and may God Himself bring you home.

June 1

You think I'm something from your imagination?
You can't begin to imagine what I am. And the sad thing
is, I wish you could. That's why God sent me. It's time
to start imagining how much He loves you.

August 1

Judging a man is easy. Compassion is hard.

June 2

People don't always have to be busy.

Sometimes they should just sit back

and enjoy the peace.

July 31

*Y*es, you made a mistake, a long time ago.

That's true. But somebody else took the truth

and twisted it into shame. God did not judge you.

Others did. They made you believe their lies. You

accepted their shame instead of God's love.

God loves you. Will you receive it?

June 3

God always gives you what you need

when you need it.

July 30

God isn't taking something away from you.
He's giving you something. It's a gift. The chance to
start over. God is there to mend your heart and heal
your soul. But you have to let Him in.

June 4

God may move in mysterious ways. But people...
their ways are the biggest mystery of all. We
can't change their past, but the good news is,
they can change where they're going.

It's time for forgiveness. Forgive. Be forgiven. And God will fill you with a peace beyond all understanding.

June 5

*W*e have to fight evil–not with our fists,

but with the power of God.

July 28

Free will is a gift. Love is a choice.

But hate leaves you no choice at all.

June 6

God can take the biggest mess and
turn it into something good.

July 27

What do you care about being loved
for your success when you're already loved
as a person and a child of God?

June 7

There's always a way out of the prisons people find themselves in.

July 26

*S*ometimes it's the simplest things that are the hardest to say...like "I'm sorry," and "I didn't mean to hurt you, I love you, we'll get through this...."

June 8

$\mathcal{W}$ho you are isn't measured by what's in your

wallet, but by what's in your soul.

July 25

Lots of people believe.

But trusting Him...that is the next step.

June 9

In heaven, eternity can be found in

but a single moment.

July 24

$\mathcal{I}$ do what I always do when I have a problem and no answers. I go into my room, turn off the lights and ask Almighty God for guidance.

June 10

Humbling yourself before your Creator and asking for advice is a sign of strength, not weakness. It suggests that in a world that demands so much of you every minute of every day, there is One who knows who you really are and loves you anyway.

July 23

I think people say terrible things to each other sometimes and they think it's too late to make things right. But you know what? That's why God invented apologies.

June 11

You must accept responsibility for the choices you made. Only then can you fully receive the forgiveness your heart needs to heal.

July 22

God wants every person to be a whole person.

A completely unique individual, not

half of someone else.

June 12

Times change, people change, interest rates change, even the land itself can change. But God is the same yesterday, today and forever.

July 21

*C*hance disappears when you make a decision.

June 13

Isn't it odd that people pray every day over the tiniest things—the weather, a green light, a baseball game, things they can't change at all. But why do people forget to pray when they are faced with a big decision? When there's a difficult choice to make, don't you think God would like to help you make it?

July 20

*I*t is not faith *in* your fathers that survives from generation to generation. It is the faith *of* your fathers. It lives here, now, and it is yours to grasp. It is the real help in times of trouble. It is the legacy your fathers have left and the gift God has given you.

June 14

God loves you. He wants to deal with what
you can do right now. Because "now"
is all you can change.

July 19

Angels don't make everything okay.

We just introduce you to the One who can.

June 15

There's nothing wrong with changing horses

midstream when the river decides

to flow the other way.

July 18

"The quality of mercy is not strained..."
Before Shakespeare said it, God was it. Mercy is His gift.
You shine with His divine light every time you
are merciful and forgive someone.

June 16

Don't give up, just keep giving.

July 17

God's not just a matchmaker. He's a matchkeeper.

June 17

$\mathcal{I}$'m not asking you to change your mind.

Just bend your heart a little.

July 16

God sees you just exactly as you are. He sees
you more perfectly and more truly than people can.
And He loves you more than you can ever imagine.

June 18

I'm ready to listen if God will give me directions,

hand me a road map, or drop me some bread crumbs.

July 15

Anybody can have a wedding.

It takes so much more to have a marriage.

That's what God wants you to have.

June 19

It's time to turn judgment into compassion.

Pain into healing. Hate into forgiveness.

July 14

*W*here there is faith, it is never too late.

June 20

God made us angels, not the police. You can hope

and pray people make the right decision,

but that's their choice, not ours.

July 13

Being a man of faith doesn't mean that you will never make mistakes. When no one else can forgive you, you know that God will. Will you let Him?

June 21

God's love never runs dry.
He can make rivers in a desert.

July 12

*W*hen you look at your children,
everything else you've done in your life
pales in comparison.

June 22

When two people choose to become one, you become something even greater than that if you ask God into the circle, "for better, for worse, for richer, for poorer." Because when times are better, God blesses you, and when times are worse, God will bless you even more.

July 11

"You can't send a letter to heaven."

"Sure you can. You don't even need paper.

You can write it with your heart."

June 23

*N*ever say never.

Sometimes the things you think'll never happen, do.

July 10

$\mathscr{T}$ruth penetrates your heart,

in a way that mere words cannot.

$\mathscr{J}$une 24

$\mathcal{G}$od didn't set this journey in motion. He's just as angry as you are that you have to walk this road. But He promises you this, He will walk this road with you. And He will be there for you when you reach the end of it. God loves you.

July 9

He will send His angels to watch over you.

June 25

Sometimes it takes a lot of courage

to keep a promise.

July 8

A family can't survive without the truth.
Now don't be afraid of the truth. Speak it,
look at it, live it.... And don't forget,
we have a choice.... Choose to love.

June 26

Forgiveness is not a sign of weakness,

it's a sign of strength.

July 7

The truth will set you free. The truth will set everybody free. But that doesn't mean it's gonna fall right into your lap. You gotta go find it first.

June 27

*A*ll the evidence in the world can still bring

a person to the wrong conclusion. But faith, faith

is the evidence of things unseen that can

only be seen by God.

July 6

*G*od doesn't make mistakes, even if the plan

is not clear to humans or angels. He knows what

He's doing; He's been doing this for years!

June 28

Love doesn't hide. It hopes all things, it endures

all things and it never fails.

July 5

*I*n this world there are two kinds of judgment: man's judgment and God's judgment. I can assure you God's judgment will be more just than anything you can imagine.

June 29

You've got to start worshiping something higher than yourself, man, 'cause I've got news for you: you are nowhere near as cool as God is.

July 4

Every day is a chance to start over, my friend.

June 30

Anyone can give up, it's the easiest thing in the world to do. But to hold it together when everyone would understand if you fell apart, that's true strength.

July 3

I'm an angel sent by God. As in Alpha Omega,

The Great I AM, the Creator of the Universe.

July 1

Don't be afraid. I'm an angel, sent by God to tell you that fear has no place in your life.

July 2